THE LOVE REPORT

Dr. Kevin Grold

ISBN-13:
978-1468132380

ISBN-10:
1468132385
Life Publications

SYNOPSIS

The Love Report explores the many facets of love.   It examines the significant questions that need to be answered if couples are ever going to fall in love and stay in love.   The meaning of love is examined not only from a therapist's, philosopher's, and poet's perspective, but more importantly from the perspective of those who actually are in love.

The Love Report challenges the reader to think about the central areas of love before presenting the answers to these modern but longstanding questions. This book is not only essential for people looking for love, but also for couples who want to enhance their relationship, and for those who think they are in love but just want to see how well they measure up.   This book is a unique and useful learning tool because it contains raw data and charts that enable readers to define their own conclusions—all with the goal of

helping you create your own long-term, love

relationship.

* * *

Do you know:

- How to be in love?

- What it means to be in love?

- How to make love last?

The Love Report will help you find the answers.

"Love, it is a high inducement to
the individual to ripen,
To become something in himself,
To become world,
To become world for himself for
another's sake,
It is a great exacting claim upon him,
Something that chooses him out and
calls him to vast things."
Rainer Maria Rilke

CONTENTS

The Roots of Love

The history of love begins in ancient times and traces the styles of loving up until the present.

What Does it Mean to be In Love?

This chapter looks at the many ways that love has been defined and focuses both upon the relationship and the expression of love.

The Background of *The Love Report*

The backgrounds of loving couples are examined with a focus on what helps and what hinders a loving relationship. It explains the different types of loving pairs and identifies the tools used to uncover the secrets of couples in love.

The Components of a Loving Relationship

This focuses on commitment and what *The Love Report* subjects are conveying when they say they are in love.

What Makes Love Last?

Being vulnerable with your partner, self-disclosure, and keeping secrets are all discussed in this chapter. It also focuses on how often couples in love need to communicate to keep their relationship strong.

What Causes Love?

Attachment, Evolution, Need Complementarity, and the Universal Love theories are discussed. This includes a look at the use of pet names and whether or not partners in love take vacations from each other.

Love: Its Problems and Solutions

This chapter examines what causes the most difficulties

for couples in love, what their parents' relationships

were like, and how couples in love solve their problems.

This chapter also includes an in-depth look at

self-esteem's relation to love.

**Finding Love in a Culture Filled with Infidelity
and Divorce**

This chapter considers how infidelity has affected the

search for love.   How do you know you have found a

partner you can trust?   This chapter examines love at

first sight and how loving couples decide they have

found their soul mate.   It includes a self-test and looks

at the direction of relationships in the future.

The New Definition of Love

This chapter combines all the information learned in *The Love Report.* It includes the history, the most up-to-date information on love, and the crucial evidence learned from *The Love Report.* It then presents an entirely new definition of love, one that will lead our society into an era of lasting, loving relationships.

The ROME Scale

This chapter presents the Relationship Openness Maturity Evaluation or ROME Scale. This is a 22 question true/false test that covers the major topics in the book. By taking this test, the reader can determine how ready he or she is to be in a lasting, loving relationship.

Lessons Learned About Love

This chapter covers the most important points to keep in mind so that you can create your own loving relationship.

Sample Profiles of *The Love Report* Subjects

The History of the Marriage Vows

FOREWORD

Having a lasting, loving relationship can be a very difficult task. However there is no challenge more important or that can provide more joy. When two people come together, there are an enormous number of complexities involved in the formation of this relationship. Unfortunately, loving relationships are rarely looked at objectively. We must move beyond guessing how to make a relationship work. What is needed is a definitive, well-researched book that will put all of the doubts, conflicts and guesses to rest. After researching couples for many years, and obtaining my Ph.D. with an emphasis on the topic of love, I compiled this information into the most complete, one-of-a-kind guidebook for anyone interested in having a lasting, loving relationship.

The research subjects, couples in love, which make up the basis for my conclusions, provide the most current consensus to help clarify this often confusing and overwhelming subject. Those of us trying to make a relationship work can now put all of our energy where it rightfully belongs - into making love happen...and, hopefully, last forever.

My sincere hope is that *The Love Report* will bring more love into your life.

~Kevin Grold Ph.D.

Del Mar, California

DEDICATION

This book is dedicated to my wife, Christine
Hartline, who has taught me that love actually can
be easy.
I Love You.   (Cancer took you from all of us much
too young.)

CHAPTER ONE:
THE ROOTS OF LOVE

Love is actually a new phenomenon for keeping relationships together. Since the beginning of human history, passion, not love, has been the driving force behind the development of relationships.   But love, for the purpose of bringing two people together, is in a stage of infancy.   We haven't learned how to master it. In fact, we haven't even learned the basic components of a mature, lasting relationship. Although we can decide that we want to be "in love," or even "fall in love," reality hits us in the face when it comes time to make a decision to have a continuing relationship.   We realize that there are no established guidelines to follow. Nobody ever taught us how to do it.   And for the most part, nobody really seems to know.

Some of us are fortunate enough to have loving parents as role models, but many of us do not have anyone to look to for guidance.   In addition, if we could find a couple or two willing to offer advice, it may not be the right advice for our situation.   What we need is a new definition of love, one that is suitable for the relationships of our current society.

To arrive at a modern definition of love, we must first look at how love has been portrayed throughout history.   By placing love in a historical context, we will be better able to look at love as a part of our heritage; a continuing part of the struggle between individuals—working to form *a more perfect union*.

A BRIEF HISTORY OF LOVE

Love originated in attraction.   If we take a historical trip back to our primitive tribal ancestors, we see that males preferred certain females.   The strongest, healthiest males demanded their choice of the most favored females within the clan - and often times they would choose several.   The females wielded power by vying for attention from the males. Those females that made themselves most desirable would attract the best males.   These ancient methods of attraction were the precursors to our modern-day love.

Our current view of love, which evolved out of this pattern, has changed dramatically throughout history.   Some of the oldest surviving records including the Egyptian hieroglyphics, contained romantic poetry that described love as the "awful curse."

Possibly the Egyptians were not actually describing something that we today would call love--because it wasn't until the Greeks that the first written exploration into the nature of love took place.   Their philosophy separated primitive sexual yearnings from the higher aims of love.   These higher aims were said to be the

pursuit of ideal beauty - not *an i*deal beauty
queen, but <u>the</u> ideal beauty of love.

Love and the Ancient Greek Culture

To the Greeks, homosexual love was love
in its highest form.   Marriage was a mere
business arrangement designed for having
children and protecting the earnings and
property of the wealthy males.   Their society
was sexist.   The husband earned a living while
the wife tended to the indoor labor such as
housecleaning and raising children.   The wife in
this arrangement was not much more than a
slave to her husband - certainly not something
that the women of today would accept.

Hesoid, a famous Greek poet, wrote:
"Get yourself a house, a woman, and a working
ox.   Buy the woman, don't marry her.   Then
you can make her plough, if necessary."

Love and the Ancient Roman Culture

With the Romans, for the first time, heterosexual love gained in popularity. The wife progressed little from her position as a slave, though she was now considered a self-respecting subject of her lord husband. She was required to do her husband's bidding sexually and otherwise. She was never to ask questions. A famous Roman senator, Metellus Numidicus, proclaimed, "If we could procreate without wives, we certainly should keep clear of that annoyance; but since nature has ordained that men can neither live happily with wives, nor at all without them, it is our duty to consider the perpetuation of the race rather than our own temporary pleasure." Love was still a long way from our modern conception.

The self-proclaimed "master of love" of this period was a poet named Ovid. He wrote an essay entitled *The Art of Love*, which had a strong influence on Roman culture. This essay

instructed Romans on how to attract a lover,
how to make love, and particularly how to
consummate adultery.   He would give men
suggestions, such as: "Tell the lady of your
desire that she has dirt on her and then brush

off her breasts, stroking them lightly as if you
are doing her a favor."   Adultery became the
accepted and even the preferred form of loving.
The idea, according to Ovid, was to keep a lover
for a short time until boredom set in, and then
to choose a new, preferably married lover.   The

divorce rate went up and the birth survival rate went down owing to crudely administered abortions and the abandoning of newborns. The disintegration of family life is said to be a main cause of the fall of the Roman Empire.

The Bible offered an answer to these "evils of society."   The Bible's fundamental law of love stated that one should "love your neighbor as yourself."   This no longer included sleeping with the neighbor's wife.   The early Church Fathers put forth the idea of celibacy and virginity.   God was married to his Chosen People.   According to the Bible, adultery was not a part of a truly loving relationship.   True love existed only in the service of God and even married couples were thought to be living in sin (marriage, in the early Church doctrine, was thought to prevent a person from serving God perfectly).   This love was an asexual, divine love where celibacy was viewed as most praiseworthy.   Sexual intercourse was only for procreation.

Since the union of marriage continued to occur, the Church took the position that they disapproved of marriages that were contracted without the wife's consent (previously only parental consent was needed).   Specifically, in 560 A.D., a prominent Christian king, Clothaire I, issued an edict that prohibited women from being married against their will.

Clothaire I

Prior to this time, marriages by capture and later, by purchase, were common.   For instance, in ancient Israel a bride was obtained by paying a "bride price" called a *mohar*. Mutual consent of both parties was symbolized by the giving of *kaseph* or money. During the ceremony, the man only needed to give his bride a *peruta*, the smallest copper coin used in Palestine, with the words "Be thou consecrated (devoted) to me." In the Middle Ages, the ceremony of giving the coin was replaced by the giving of a plain ring.

Development Of Courtly Love

In Languedoc (southern France), a form of love, unprecedented in western civilization, was born. Many knights found themselves living in the castles of southern France, with only one lady, the wife of the lord of the castle. This lady of the castle utilized her etiquette and manners to keep these virile young men in line. The more crude and forward the men were, the more she kept them at a distance. It didn't take long for the more intelligent men to realize that refinement and courtesy were the way to this idealized woman's favor.

Men began to copy the patterns of a feudal vassal submitting to his lord. They went to great lengths to show their adoration. The troubadours of the time began to cultivate the arts of singing, dancing, and composing poetry to please the ladies of their desire. These knights took vows of faith, they squandered their money, and even engaged in chivalrous, life-threatening jousts to win the favor of their loved ones - all of which became known as Courtly Love.

(The marriage ceremony itself became an attempt to imitate the courtly marriages of kings and queens with the bridal gowns emulating a queen's royal dress and the bridesmaids and groomsmen emulating the royal court — a tradition which carries on in many marriages today.)

Eleanor, Queen of France, had a strong influence on the development of Courtly Love. She gathered knights, ladies, and poets around her and created an elegant court. Here, issues of love including chivalry, table manners, courtesy, and love-making were both taught and created.

In mock-legal proceedings, a lover could present a complaint and defense regarding a matter of love. A jury of women handed down their decision which became a new part of the Courtly code of ethics.

Prior to this time, marriage was viewed as a tool for men to enrich themselves. Men would obtain a dowry and then proceed to

annul the marriage.   The ladies of the court

would not stand for this - but they did not rule

in favor of marriage as one might expect.

Instead, they ruled in favor of love.

To decide on an issue of Courtly Love, the
question was posed: "Can true love exist
between married people?"
The Judgment: It cannot.

In 1174, the Countess Marie of

Champagne (daughter of Eleanor), ruled in the

court of love in Poitiers, that love was a free and mutual expression of emotion whereas marriage was a duty.   Marriage was found to be incompatible with the freedom necessary for love; adultery was proclaimed as the true manner of expressing love.   Marie of Champagne had one of her clergy, Andreas Capellanus, write down the results of these court proceedings.   His book, *The Art of Courtly Love*, classified the adulterous manners into thirty-one basic rules of Courtly Love.   These included the ideas that jealousy is a necessary part of love; that the lover should always have the beloved in mind, and that loving two people at the same time is impossible.   His book became the sole instruction manual on love and caused adultery to flourish throughout Europe.

During the Renaissance period, the nature of family life changed and more time was spent in the cities.   For the first time, the beginnings of modern marriage could be seen in the rise of the importance of the idea that young couples should live apart from their families in a home of their own. The concept of smaller family units began to take hold which resulted in an increased time at home as a couple. The desirability of one's longer-term marriage partner, over and above the dowry, now became important. Couples who lived together were considered married by canon law (the rules of the Christian Church), and the dowry became the symbol of an honorable marriage.

Being an honorable member of society continued to rise in importance. The marriage vows of this time reflected this rise in that they now included a statement that declared marriage to be "ordained for a remedy against sin, to avoid fornication, that such persons as have not the gift of continency (celibacy), that they should marry and keep themselves

undefiled members of Christ's body."
(Consultation, 1536)

In the year 1563 at the Council of Trent, the Church Fathers declared that a marriage was not to be considered valid unless it was accompanied by a priest in the presence of two or three witnesses.   Before this time, marriages occurred without any ceremony and were frowned upon by the Church.

Surprisingly, the priestly benediction (ceremony) is not found in either the Christian Bible or in the Jewish Talmud as one might expect.   The creation of the marriage ceremony is left entirely to the person in charge of marrying the couple.   The customary practice, started in the middle sixteenth century, was to follow the matrimonial rules listed in the *Book of Common Prayer*.   This book popularized the "for better and for worse" version of the marriage vows and the ideal of commitment to one spouse.   (Note: The

Christian priest's duties were not only restricted to the vows, but were also considered, at that time, to be the blessing of the bridal bed to bring the couple a long life and healthy children. See Appendix 2 for an in-depth look at the marriage vows.)

This quick historical jaunt finally arrives at the New World. Here we find that the Puritans valued marriage highly and specifically, sex within the context of marriage (Martin Luther argued that celibacy was invented by the Devil). Sex outside of marriage, and especially adultery, were considered serious sins that frequently led to excommunication.

Women returned to being subordinate to their husbands but no longer as a worker-slave. They were now told to devote themselves to home-making in an atmosphere of emotional harmony. Marriage was considered a necessary domestic arrangement to satisfy the man's needs for food, clothing, children, status, and even, sex.   (The strict

morals of the Puritans belong to a later period -

the middle 18th century.)

From the middle of the seventeenth

century, the Age of Reason, and on into the

Enlightenment of the eighteenth century,

intellect was promoted above any emotion -

including love.   Women were supposed to keep

their mind and body in a state of perfection

through proper training and directed reading.

Men wanted educated women so they could

carry on a conversation.   But women were not

to be *too* educated - only smart enough to tell a

good man by his character so they would not

"mistakenly fall in love with the butler."

Love was considered a matter of natural

sexual desire.   These desires were confined to

a new manner of relating called Gallantry.

Gallantry was a set of carefully rehearsed

manners designed to apply logic to relationships

and to conceal feelings.   Maintaining icy

self-control was ideal while the display of ritualized politeness demonstrated good breeding and reason. Love, reduced to mere sensuality, became a malicious game of seduction and desertion. (This was exemplified in the movie "Dangerous Liaisons.") "Marry an older woman", it was said; because the older woman would be discreet when having an affair and would not tarnish one's reputation (this guidance came from none other than Benjamin Franklin).

Gallantry at its best. From the movie Dangerous Liasions, a Lorimar Film.

The control of one's emotions began to wane in popularity toward the end of the eighteenth century. A new form of love became popular that emphasized the search for a pure emotional experience - an experience that transcended ordinary sexual relations. It was known as Romantic Love. This type of love was an attempt to experience the unity or "oneness" of the universe with the joining of two souls. The idea was that every person has certain deficiencies that can be made whole through joining with a soul mate – one whose assets complement their liabilities. If a person finds the right match then a wondrous experience of unity is the result.

Romantic love turned out to be destructive to the institution of marriage because this view of love encouraged adultery over commitment and attacked "loveless" marriages by fostering the idea that if the relationship was not working perfectly, then one should continue the search for the "ideal" union.

In the nineteenth century, the reaction to the destruction of the institution of marriage fostered a new form of love: Victorian love. Again, love as a valued emotion became popular within the institution of marriage.   Although marriage and love became important factors in society, sexuality was avoided and a shy, reserved manner of courtship appeared.   Sex was not to be enjoyed.   Extreme sexual fears and taboos became a main part of daily life. Society dictated that it was everyone's duty to be a virgin until marriage.   After marriage, sex was considered dangerous if it occurred more than once a month.   No wonder Freud attributed all psychological problems to a frustrated sexual desire.   Love was no exception.   Freud saw love as deriving out of sexual impulses that were not able to be fulfilled.

The women's movement helped women see that they did not need to remain in unhappy marriages.   In the United States, between 1870 and 1905, the divorce rate grew three times faster than the population.   Women, for the first time, demanded satisfaction in their relationships, not only emotionally, but also sexually - the days of having to endure forced sex from their husbands were gone.   No longer were relationships held together by the hardships of frontier life or religious or social traditions, now they were expected to be held together by love.

Women began setting aside days to have men "call" on them at home.   Tea and cakes would be served in the parlor and then the young man and woman would play the piano or sit on the porch - all in full earshot of the family. If more than a few dates on a woman's calendar became filled with one man, they were said to be "dating."

Around the beginning of the 20th century, dating took on its own meaning.   It now meant that a man would take a woman out of the house for a special occasion such as going to the theater.   In contrast to calling, the dating man was expected to pay for all of the entertainment. Since the family was no longer able to effectively chaperone, outings such as car dates would often lead to *spooning* (later called necking, and then, making out).

"The perfect family"

Dating became the common means of selecting a spouse.   People required years of practice experimenting with various partners and "commitments" to find one's soul mate. This new view of love attempted the difficult balancing act of trying to combine a sexual outlet, a procreative function, and a close emotional connection.

Romance novels and, later, movies and television fostered the idea that two young, beautiful people would suddenly "fall madly in love," which led to the inevitable "living happily ever after."   (These fairy tales never mentioned the idea of working on a relationship complete with the tasks of living together and creating a family which have led to unrealistic and damaging expectations.)   Unfortunately, many people looked to these ideal relationships for role models and guidance only to be greatly disappointed.

The nineteen-sixties found many people disillusioned with this new concept of love. New birth control methods emerged such as *the pill* and the younger generation turned toward "Free Love."   This was the idea that a person could genuinely love (or have sex with) more than one person at the same time.

During the seventies, divorces continued to rise until one out of every two marriages were unsuccessful.   Jealousies and complications grew to the point where many people realized that intensely loving more than one person at a time was very difficult.

During the eighties, deadly sexually transmitted diseases such as AIDS encouraged a more serious interest in monogamous relationships.   Promiscuity became a game of deadly sexual roulette.   Churches even began requiring couples to attend sanctioned pre-marital counseling before being married. Generally, people began attempting to pair up with the hope that love would keep them together.

Today, relationships are in turmoil and couples are struggling to define relationships for themselves. Clearly understanding the goal that so many individuals have of "being in love," in the context of history will help to bring this love experience to fruition.

This quick and abridged version of the history of love shows that the definition and meaning of love is not constant. Before I learned about the history of love, I thought that love was the same now as it always had been.

I did not realize that many times throughout history adultery was considered a part of love, or that sex was considered separate from love, or that homosexual love was once considered the common form of love. Through the following chapters we will see the development of a new type of love; a definition of love that derives from couples who have

Courtly Love	Chivalry, Adultery, Jealousy
Gallantry	Manners, Logic & Seduction
Romantic Love	Joining of two soul mates
Victorian Love	Shy, Reserved Courtship

grown and matured in healthy relationships.   A love will be revealed that is not only suitable for our times, but more importantly, a guide for the future.

NOTE: This short history of love cannot cover everyone in western society (over a span of several centuries) in just a few sentences.

When I say that the "fifties couples were very conservative," or that the sixties couples were into "free love," these are generalities. Hopefully this information will germinate your interest and spur you on to learn more about each of these interesting times in our brief history of love.

CHAPTER TWO: WHAT DOES IT MEAN TO BE IN LOVE?

Do you want to be in love?   If you do, then you have to understand exactly what it means to be "in love."   For instance, would you be satisfied with a loving relationship that lasted for only a day, a week, or even a year?   If you had this limited experience and then it went away, would you still be happy that you had been in love?   The chances are that you want to be in love forever and this is a very difficult and challenging accomplishment.

The word love is used in so many creative ways that it can cause confusion for anyone using it to express a feeling.   For instance, notice the following definitions of love.   Which one most closely matches your way of thinking? Do you define love as a combination of those listed or perhaps something unique?

DEFINITIONS OF LOVE

(Derived from Greek and Roman literature)

Agape or Caritas........Love devoted toward the welfare of others.

Eros...........................Sexual Love

Ludus.........................Playful Love

Philia.........................Brotherly, Affectionate Love

Storge.......................Tenderness and Companionship

Mania.......................Frenzied Passion

One of the first objectives in learning to have a loving relationship is to obtain a clear definition of love.

WHAT IS LOVE?

When looking at the definition of love, not only do we need to explore the expression of love (as in the above historical definitions), but also the *relationship* involved.

For example, a loving experience can develop out of the relationship between parents and their children.   Another love develops from the inner bond between family members (despite the popularity of sibling rivalry).   The word is also used to describe how one feels about art, or nature, or such things as their favorite possession.   Then there is the love between friends, or the love you have for your pets.   And finally, there is the love for God (or a higher power).

These expressions of love all represent unconditional emotions of love that continue to passively exist at some level despite problems and challenges.   With all of these varieties, it is easy to see how any one definition can quickly become confused with love—the love used to describe a couple's relationship.

The focus of *The Love Report* is ONLY the love between two people who start out as strangers and work to create a unity from their separate backgrounds, styles, and ideas. Relationships are hard enough to cultivate and maintain without additional confusion and distraction in our thoughts and words.   If we reserve the word LOVE for the unique experience between two people in a relationship, then one easy obstacle is removed.

♥ ♥

CHAPTER THREE: THE BACKGROUND OF THE LOVE REPORT

So where do we begin?   Many people say that the best thing to do when faced with a difficult task is to obtain the finest advice available from those who have already traveled down the road before you.   As I mentioned in chapter one, there are not many good role models for how to be in love.   Our society currently has a divorce rate over fifty percent. This means that more than one out of every two marriages ends in divorce.   Our society has no method for teaching the necessary social skills required to succeed in the demanding job of "committed partner."   So what should we do? For starters, we **could** go to the bookstore and read all of the books in the psychology section pertaining to relationships.   But there is a fatal flaw in this reasoning.   These therapists are well versed in the study of human behavior (I should know, I have a Ph.D. in Psychology) and love is certainly a human behavior.   But, unfortunately the typical psychologist (or any therapist) is trained to help others deal with PROBLEMS.   In fact, 99.9 percent of the literature upon which therapeutic theories are based is centered on helping people cope with their negative issues.

Take another look at the books in the psychology section at the bookstore.   Turn the book over and look at the author's credentials. You will find something like this: "I have been a couple's counselor for over 10 years and have helped thousands of people effectively combat their emotional problems."   There is that word again.   The question you must ask yourself is: Do you want your future love relationship based on the experience of other people having problems?   Most likely your answer is no.

When I found out that the authors of my favorite book on "How to have a loving relationship" were getting a divorce, I decided that there must be some other answer to the question of how to successfully be in a loving relationship.

I then studied journals in the library and found that there was some research on love! Unfortunately, it was based (as is a great deal of psychological research) on college freshmen. Seventeen and eighteen year-olds are not the best role models for how to have a lasting, loving relationship.   Besides, even if they were in a long-term relationship, how long could it have been?

Instead, what if there was a large group of couples who had successfully created a relationship without any outside counseling? Then, we would all want to know, "What's *their* secret?"

I decided to conduct my own research by surveying couples who have made a relationship work over many years. This was the essential information that was lacking for those of us working toward a lasting, loving relationship.

Before my research could begin, there were a number of things that I required. Obviously, I needed couples in love. So I placed advertisements in two national newspapers. I also asked friends to help out and discovered that almost everybody, if they tried hard enough, could think of at least one couple that had a loving relationship. Eventually, I had a large database of couples from fourteen different states.

One hundred and six couples were chosen. These couples averaged 45 years in age, were together in their relationship an average of 17 years, and came from all across the United States. They came from Florida to Washington State, from Texas to Kansas, from

California to New York, and many other states in-between. There were bankers, homemakers, factory workers, doctors, farmers, realtors, and a few couples who were struggling by in this economy unemployed. The selected "in love" couples were from all walks of life.

But what if these couples answered my survey thinking they were in love, but were as confused as most other people as to what "in love" really meant? I needed a way to separate those couples who felt an intensely positive "love" emotion for their partners from those that did not.

As an example, one man contacted me from Texas saying enthusiastically that he and his wife were deeply in love and would I please send a questionnaire. But instead of him completing it and sending it back, his wife of thirty-four years returned the survey without answering any questions, saying: "He only cares about himself."

It became obvious that people just telling me that they were in love was not enough. A method was needed to scientifically conclude that they *were* in love.   Fortunately, I found a test that had been well established over the years among love researchers for determining whether or not a person is in love: the Rubin Love Scale, devised by Zick Rubin, Ph.D.

Now, I had both a large number of couples who told me that they were in love and a tool to determine which couples really loved each other.

The Rubin Love Scale

By using the Rubin Love Scale as a barometer, it became clear that the couples who stated that they were in love, actually fell into three categories: (1) BALANCED LOVE - those couples with both partners strongly in love; (2) UNBALANCED LOVE - those couples with only one partner strongly in love; and (3) NON-LOVE - those couples with neither partner experiencing a strong, loving emotion.

Even though every couple that I studied for *The Love Report* declared that they were in love, this "balance factor" helped to clarify what makes up a *mutual*, loving relationship.   Also, those couples who had been together for more than five years were compared to those who were in an earlier phase of their relationship. (Five years was the dividing line used in the marital research.)   If there was a difference between the advice of those who were in a lasting, loving relationship and the advice of those just starting out, then clearly it made sense to follow the advice of the couples who had been together longer.

The Love Report Filters

Thus, *The Love Report,* in narrowing the qualifications of those who could present useful advice, uncovered three "advice filters:" those in love vs. those not in love; those in a balanced relationship from those who were either in an

Balanced Love, Unbalanced Love, and Non-Love But they all say, "We are in love."

unbalanced or a non-love situation; and those who had made their relationship last for more than five years compared with those who had not been together for that long.   These advice filters provided *The Love Report* with the tools to uncover the rarely revealed secrets of loving couples.

My presentation of these results begins with an in-depth look at the background of the subjects who were selected.

The Love Report: Analysis and Data

Length of Time Together

* Number of subjects with less than five years together= 58

* Number of subjects with more than five years together = 154

These couples break down into the following categories:

106 were together for more than 10 years

44 were together for more than 30 years

6 were together for more than 50 years

Education Completed

* Number of subjects:

Less than 12th grade	= 3
High school	= 26
Some college	= 58
Bachelors degree	= 63
Masters degree	= 29
Doctorate	= 25

Income Level

* Number of subjects:

Less than $10,000/yr	= 3
$10,000-$16,999/yr	= 13
$17,000-$22,999/yr	= 31
$30,000-$49,999/yr	= 43
$50,000-$75,999/yr	= 48
$76,000 or more	= 51
Declined to answer	= 14

Size of the Town

* Number of subjects:

Less than 10,000 people	= 17
10,000-50,000 people	= 54
50,001-250,000 people	= 37
More than 250,000 people	= 90

Age of the Subjects

* Number of subjects:

<u>Age</u>

Less than 20 years	= 1
20-29	= 41
30-39	= 53
40-49	= 43
50-59	= 24
60-69	= 19
70-79	= 23
80 or greater	= 2

(Average Age = 44.59 years)

Previous Relationships

* Number of relationships (that lasted at least 6 months):

Relationships	Subjects
0	75
1	48
2	38
3	23
4	17
5	2
6	5
7	2
8	1
30	1

*   *   *

From these statistics we can draw some important conclusions: (1) you do not have to be rich to be in love; (2) you do not have to have a degree to be in love; and (3) you do not have to live in large city or town.   In addition, race and religion had no identifiable influence upon the "love experience."   But what did make a difference was marital status.

Marital Status

Married couples' average love test score was 96.39 and unmarried couples' average love test score was 90.67 (From the Rubin Love Scale).

The research showed that married couples are significantly more in love than those who are not married.   Gender also made a difference. Males scored higher (or more in love) on the survey questions than their female counterparts.

Male average love test score= 96.85
Female average love test score= 93.06

The Love Report research concludes that males are more intense in their loving relationships than their female counterparts. This may be because males are less able to commit to a relationship.   Once they do commit, their experience becomes stronger. This male/female difference will be discussed further in the chapters ahead.

♥ ♥

CHAPTER FOUR:
THE COMPONENTS OF
A LOVING
RELATIONSHIP

How is love able to keep a couple together?   Love has not always been the basis for the joining of two people.   For hundreds of years individuals were brought together in marriages that were arranged for traditional, political, religious, and financial reasons.   For example, if you lived several centuries ago, on your fourteenth birthday you would meet your life-long spouse chosen for you by your elders. For some cultures, this is still the case today.

In our modern, western society, people still occasionally marry for financial reasons, but the family unit is no longer held together by small town pressures, religious sanctions, and tradition.   Love is hoped to be the cement that binds couples together.   Even though today

love does not work as well as it could, research

confirms that whether or not a couple is in love

provides the single most effective predictor of

the long-term success of a relationship.

A compilation of the latest published

love research revealed six primary areas that the

experts considered fundamental to a couple in a

mature state of love.

The Six Predicted Components of Love

(A) Romance

(B) Passion & Sex

(C) Commitment to be together

(D) Self Disclosure/Communication

(E) Spiritual Growth & Learning

(F) Learning about yourself through being in the

relationship

Unfortunately, none of these experts

could agree as to which of the components were

most important.   *The Love Report* subjects were asked to rank these topics in order of importance to them.

How would *you* order these six topics in terms of importance to love?
Decide now before reading further.

(C) Commitment to be Together was by far the most frequent selection.   The second most important selection was (D) Self Disclosure/ Communication.   These two responses were followed by (A) Romance, (E) Spiritual Growth and Learning, (B) Passion and Sex, and in last position (F) Learning about yourself through being in the relationship.

Imagine what a different view of love we would have if the couples in love discovered romance and passion as the primary factors of their relationships.

With so much confusion about love today,

it is useful to further examine these findings.

Many people, including some prominent love

researchers, do not view commitment as

important to the meaning of love (especially not

the most important factor).   "You can love more than one person at a time," and "I love my girlfriend and my wife" are just two of the many common statements from people that lack this one person commitment.

This *Report* determined that commitment is the foundation of a continuing, loving relationship.   In addition, when the Balanced Love couples (the couples with both partners strongly in love) were compared with the Unbalanced couples (with only one partner strongly in love) and Non-Love Couples (neither partner strongly in love), it became clear that the more Balanced a couple is, the more likely they were to rate commitment as the most important aspect of their relationship.

Even though many people feel commitment is a significant part of their relationship, it does not mean that they have defined or discussed what that commitment means.   (In an informal poll of some couples, not a part of this survey, I found that the

participants all firmly believed in commitment

but fewer than 10% said that they had taken the

time to actually discuss the meaning of that

commitment.)

To compare the few couples I informally

polled with the couples in love from this *Report*,

the subjects were asked the following question:

TO WHAT EXTENT HAVE YOU VERBALIZED A
COMMITMENT TO YOUR PARTNER?

(A) We have no commitment.

(B) Never discussed the commitment but it is
implied.

(C) Discussed commitment briefly but not
thoroughly.

(D) Have thoroughly discussed commitment.

The results revealed a different pattern
from the couples that I informally polled.   Most
of the subjects, 77%, said they had thoroughly
discussed their commitment.

"Do you understand Latin?"

Only 14% said that they had discussed it briefly, and even less, 8%, said that they had never discussed their commitment.   (Less than 6% had no commitment.)   In conclusion, the research subjects said that a thorough discussion about commitment was vital to their relationship.

To obtain an in-depth look at the meaning of commitment, I reviewed published literature specifically in this area and found that there were several definitions set forth by the current experts.   I combined these main ideas and asked my subjects to rank the following statements in terms of importance:

The Five Predicted Aspects of Commitment

(A) Agree to stay together no matter what.
(B) Agree to have a sexually exclusive relationship.

(C) Agree to communicate our thoughts and feelings honestly.

(D) Agree to live up to our religious beliefs and values.

(E) Agree to help make our relationship an active process where we both strive to make it better.

Again, before you read on, ask yourself how you would order the previous list in terms of importance.

The two definitions that tied for first place were (E) Agree to help make our relationship an active process where we both strive to make it better, and (C) Agree to communicate our thoughts and feelings honestly. Right in the middle of the group was (B) Agree to have a sexually exclusive relationship.

There was a tie for last place. Both (D) Agree to live up to our religious beliefs and values, and (A) Agree to stay together no matter what fell significantly below the other responses. Even though commitment has traditionally meant, "I will stay with you no matter what," *The Love Report* couples clearly defined commitment differently by selecting this choice as the last among five.

The following are typical examples of how the subjects described their commitment:

Jo, a housewife married for 16 years viewed commitment this way: *"A large part of love and staying together is commitment. Commitment means being dedicated and loyal to the growth of oneself, one's partner and the relationship between the two. It means choosing for the benefit of all three, not just one."*

Conversely, Marleen, a housewife married for 24 years, said: *"Commitment means that I am faithful to him sexually as well as emotionally. I don't open myself up to becoming seriously involved with anyone else. I am committed to trying to form a close relationship with him and not run away when there are difficulties."*

Roger, an unemployed carpenter currently looking for work, added: *"Commitment means remaining true to the pledge we made to each other - stated or implied - through good times and bad. Commitment means following through on what you have given your partner reason to expect."*

It is clear that love is not something that just happens. Instead, it is a creation of two people working together to understand each other and their relationship. People who are not "in love" significantly more often define commitment as staying together no matter what. This fact is associated with insecurities and the fear of being alone. Even so, often with a boost in self-esteem, these people come to recognize that they deserve a relationship equal to the emotional investment they are willing to make.

Commitment is the turning point between searching for a compatible mate, and maintaining a mature relationship. It means more than let's not have sex with anyone else. Commitment begins with a statement of intent to continue the relationship over time. But this commitment is not something to be declared and then left alone. It is a process. As people grow together and change, so does the relationship.

Therefore, a commitment is a bond developed to maintain a connected relationship within that growing process. Commitment also entails taking an interest in your partner's well being and letting your partner know that his or her life will continue as a central concern. Once this type of commitment has begun, a secure environment is created that enables intimacy to progress.

CHAPTER FIVE: WHAT MAKES LOVE LAST?

When you create a love relationship, it is natural to encounter problems.   Yet, how do you know if these challenges are rooted in fundamental differences between you and your partner, or merely in the way you are communicating?   How do you know if you are communicating too much or not enough?
In other words, how do you evaluate the effectiveness of your communication?

Self-Disclosure

The answer is straightforward.
Effective communication is rooted in self-disclosure.   Saying the things that are personal and difficult to say is the key to creating intimacy.   No other single statement

concerning relationship satisfaction has the backing of *The Love Report* results than this statement.   Think to yourself what would be the hardest thing to say to your partner (or future partner)?   Now, picture your partner listening and accepting you the way that you are with what you have said.   How would you feel?

Self-disclosure helps build trust.   It fosters intimacy.   In turn this enables better understanding of your partner.   Better understanding helps avert dysfunctional communication and unnecessary problems. The act of sharing and being vulnerable with your partner helps to clarify your perception of your own personality.   By doing so, your partner will not only understand you better, but will also be more likely to follow your lead.

Being vulnerable is the key to intimacy. The most loving couples are those who are most willing to share intimate details with each other.

"Sharing your fears brings the
relationship together"

The Love Report subjects provided
interesting insights into the relationship
between love and self-disclosure when they
answered the following question:

DO YOU BELIEVE THAT WE SHOULD BOTH:

(A) Be willing to tell each other everything about ourselves and have no secrets?

(B) Tell each other most things and keep some things private?

(C) Only tell our partner those things about our past that would not be disturbing to our partner?

The largest percentage (61%) of the subjects chose (B) To keep some things private. Only 30% choose (A) To have no secrets, and only 9% chose (C) Only tell your partner things that would not be disturbing.

The subjects were then asked to be more specific by answering the following question:

WHAT PERCENT OF THE PERSONAL ASPECTS OF YOURSELF ARE YOU WILLING TO SHARE?

Surprisingly, only a small percentage (28%) said that they would share 100% of their personal aspects.   Fortunately, for those who are interested in having an intimate relationship, another 27% said that they would share 99% percent of their personal lives.   About 25% of the subjects chose a category that stated they would only share 90% or less of their personal lives with their partner.   The results show that not everyone in a loving relationship shares 100% of their personal lives.

This seeming contradiction was explained by the fact that many of the people that I interviewed said they were willing to share intimate details with their partners but they had learned to keep things to themselves that would be hurtful.

Laurence, a retired doctor married for 45 years, said: "*There are many incidents in my history that, while they helped to form the person I now am, belong to the person I was then;*

74

almost a complete other being. As such, while I don't deny them, neither do I embrace or disclose them."

The Balanced Love Couples (both partners strongly in love) answered they were more likely to share 99% of themselves, while the Unbalanced Love Couples (one partner strongly in love) and Non-Love Couples (neither partner strongly in love) significantly more often chose to share only 75% or less.   This demonstrates that the more Balanced a couple is (both partners strongly in love); the more they are willing to self-disclose.

To examine your compatibility, try the Grold Love Test smartphone app available online.

How much do you disclose?

The subjects were then asked this question:

IF YOU HAD A CONSTANT THOUGHT OR FEELING

THAT YOUR PARTNER WOULD DISAPPROVE OF

OR THAT WOULD CAUSE YOUR PARTNER

DISTRESS, WOULD YOU TELL YOUR PARTNER?

(A) Never

(B) Most likely not

(C) Probably

(D) Yes

Sixty percent said (C) Probably or (D) Yes, while forty percent said (A) Never or (B) Most likely not.

I was rather disappointed in the subjects' responses to the last two questions. I had hoped that people would be more disclosing, until I examined the data more closely.

When the "in love" group was compared to the "not in love" group, it became very clear that those more in love do share a much greater percentage of the personal aspects of themselves than those not in love. Also, those in love are more likely **not** to keep secrets from their partner.

Teri, a housewife married for 32 years, said: "*The most intimate thing in my life that I have the most trouble sharing with my partner has to do with sex. But with my partner's encouragement, I have been as open and honest as I can. It was more difficult for me to tell him, than it was for him to hear it.*"

The Love Report data shows that the more in love a couple is, the more willing they are to share their personal lives together.

Jack, a retail clerk married for 30 years expressed: "*I don't think there is anything or any area that I can't discuss with Camile - that's one of the special things in our relationship...to trust someone that I can freely share with and find*

understanding."

To more clearly outline the components of a lasting, loving relationship, the couples were next asked to clarify their communication styles by answering this question:

HOW OFTEN DO YOU AND YOUR PARTNER DISCUSS INTIMATE ISSUES?

(A) Once a day.

(B) Once a week.

(C) Once a month.

(D) Once a year.

(E) Never.

The largest percentage said that they discussed intimate issues (B) Once a week.   This was followed by (A) Once a day; (C) Once a month; (D) Once a year; and then (E) Never.

I analyzed the data further and found those in love more often discuss intimate issues once a day than those not in love.

Likewise, the Balanced Love Group were more likely to discuss intimate issues once a day while the Unbalanced and Non-love Groups were more likely to discuss intimate issues once a week.

Carole, a retired banker married for 34 years said: *"Sharing the intimate details of our everyday life is not only essential, but the basis*

"You're not hearing me!"

of our growing relationship. We make an effort to talk together everyday about our feelings, concerns, and anything that upsets each other. If we don't, a pressure builds up and eventually there's an explosion. I've learned that it's much better to take off the pressure on a daily basis."

Unfortunately, many people do not know how to communicate effectively. Intimate communication, in specific, is a necessary skill to learn in order to thrive in an intimate relationship. One of the most common difficulties that couples have in trying to communicate is that they do not use "I statements." "I statements" are direct statements of how you are feeling such as: "I felt ignored at the party." Instead of, "You talked to everyone at the party, except me!" The second type of communication is a "You" statement. These "You" statements can lead to increased difficulties instead of increased understanding.

Another important listening skill is the ability to repeat back the communication your partner has said to you.   The idea is to repeat the information exactly as it was intended without adding any answers, comments, or suggestions.   Then you ask the person communicating if you repeated the information correctly.   If so, the dialogue can continue.   If not, then you have to try again until you can repeat back what your partner has said to his or her satisfaction.

These basic communication skills may sound simple but they are not easy. Frequently, during dialogue, issues from the past will surface and unrelated concerns will interfere.   This is why it is important to have a good understanding of your own issues so you can recognize when they are obstructing your relationship.

A helpful suggestion: If you and your partner are *continually* having trouble discussing issues, then seek professional assistance to improve your communication.   A third party professional can make a big difference in your ability to share your feelings and communicate with your partner.

A relationship will last and grow when you put energy into it.   One way to do that is through romance.   Romance was ranked third (in the last chapter) after commitment and self-disclosure in terms of the most important components of love.   Therefore, taking the time to show your partner that he or she is the most important person in the world kindles the fire of love and expands the joy of being together.   When romance is combined with taking a risk and sharing intimate feelings and fears with regular, open communication, then love will last and flourish.

CHAPTER SIX: WHAT CAUSES LOVE TO HAPPEN?

In ancient times, the Greeks and Romans believed that if a person was to hold some *erithraicon*, a special plant, then he or she would be overtaken with a lustful desire.   Hercules, as the legend states, is said to have deflowered 50 daughters of Thespius in one night after consuming the root of this plant.   The mandrake root is another substance that has been used throughout history as a primary ingredient in love potions.   It was thought to stimulate strong sexual desire, increase potency in males, and cure female sterility.   Over time, countless substances have been tried as an aphrodisiac, but in *The Love Report*, we want to examine the causes of feeling in love from the perspective of those purposefully creating a relationship.

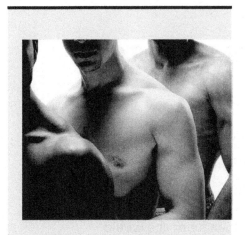

I will take THAT one!

The Love Report has already determined that the person that you feel in love with should be willing to communicate openly, be willing to make a commitment (remember we are talking about love - not infatuation), should have similar values, interests, and goals, and there should be an inner feeling that you both "connect."

Obviously, you do not fall in love with every person you meet.   So how do you select a partner?   Some people believe that it is fate or divine intervention that causes two soul mates to find each other.   But falling in love requires opening yourself to a mature relationship that involves both sharing and commitment.   This assumes that you are not currently involved in an unfulfilling but committed liaison and that you are not spending all of your time dating people that really don't interest you.

However, many single people spend a great deal of their free time desperately searching for the so-called "right one."   Their fruitless search creates disappointment and misery that fuels desperation.   This desperation is hard to hide and turns others away.   If instead, they spent their time engaging in activities with others that they enjoy, then their enjoyment would create a contagious energy and finding a soul mate would happen naturally and easily.

Although it is an important and vast topic for discussion, whether or not divine intervention plays a role in finding love, is best left for the religious philosophers to deliberate and report.

What creates an attraction between two people has been widely studied by social psychologists.   They have shown people are attracted to individuals who have similar attitudes, beliefs, athletic abilities, intelligence, and physical characteristics.   But out of all of the choices of partners, what causes love to happen with just that one special person?

Many theories have been devised to describe how partners are selected, but these theories are difficult to compare and visualize because the mechanisms of selection are thought to work unconsciously.

I will share with you my findings about the four most prominent theories while you decide which one might be applicable for your situation.

ATTACHMENT THEORY

Attachment theorists consider love to serve the function of re-creating our lost infantile experience.   The idea is that people are trying to re-experience the warm, dreamy comfort they once had (or wish they had) when they were continually cared for by their mother. These theorists point out that the contact-maintaining behaviors of infants, which include, caressing, smiling, rocking, kissing, holding, and making eye contact are the same behaviors displayed by adult lovers.   The tenderness displayed in response to helplessness, vulnerabilities, or the tears of the partner, these theorists say, provides evidence of this innate reaction.   They view people in love as needing approval from their partner and feeling very upset by their partner's absence.

These theorists also point to the use of pet names by those in love as evidence that people are trying to re-create the experience of their parents calling them childlike names when they were young.   To find out more about this idea, *The Love Report* subjects were asked if they use pet names.   The findings showed that most subjects *do* use pet names.   Two answers tied as the most popular response: (A) I continually use pet names, and (B) I occasionally use pet names.   These were followed by (C) I never use pet names, and (D) I used pet names in the past, but not any more.

Honey, Sweetheart, Sweetie, Pie (short for Sweetie Pie), Love, Vixen, Lolly, Bunny, Sugar, Hudgie, and Daddy are some of the best examples that subjects provided.   Most of the subjects (78%) responded that they do use pet names at least occasionally, which lends credence to the attachment theory.   Only a small group (17%) of the subjects responded that they do not use pet names and never did. In addition, length of the relationship may have some tie to using pet names since couples who have been together for more than five years were much less likely to use pet names.

Another area of focus for attachment theory is separation anxiety. Attachment theorists believe that just as a baby is distressed when a mother leaves it, so too are couples distressed when they are apart. Contrary to this notion, some couples actually create time apart from each other. Is this healthy, or does it signal trouble in a relationship? I asked the research couples to find out where they stood on this issue with the following question:

FROM THESE THREE CHOICES, HAVE YOU EVER SET ASIDE A SPECIFIC TIME TO BE APART FROM YOUR PARTNER? (e.g., separate vacations)

   (A) Except for our jobs we are basically never apart.
   (B) I will occasionally do things to be apart

from my partner for short periods of
time (less than 1 day).

(C) I set aside time apart from my partner
(more than 1 day).

The research revealed that the two
opposites (A) We are basically never apart (26%),
and (C) I set aside time to be away from my
partner for more than one day (25%) are
essentially ranked the same, and therefore does
not lead to any specific conclusions.   The
response (B) I will do things apart from my
partner for less than one day was chosen about
twice as often as either of the previously
mentioned choices (49%).

In essence, there was no evident,
unidirectional answer from these results as to
whether or not the attachment theory and,
specifically, anxiety from separation, gave a
clear and final answer as to why individuals fall
in love. However, when those "in love" were

compared to those "not in love" and the Balance Factor was examined, a different answer was forthcoming.

Those that scored "in love" stated that they DID NOT spend more than one day apart from their partner while those that scored "not in love" significantly more often stated that they did take some time away from their partner for more than one day.

The Balanced Love couples also showed this same pattern.   They were more likely to choose not to spend time apart from their partners as compared to the NON-Love couples. These responses demonstrate that the more in love you are, the less likely you are to spend time apart from your partner.

Darleen, an interior designer married for 12 years, stated: "*If we could spend 24 hours a day together I surely would!   As long as we find time to do our hobbies (his karate, my yoga), I think we'd be in the same house together.   But we both work so there is a lot of time apart which makes us very happy to be together. We find that if there are too many busy days where we do not get our alone time in then we get irritable.*" Her husband Rick, a painter, added: "*We're very conscious of keeping at least one day a week for ourselves, just to play together (movies, shopping, dinner, adventures, etc.) - no friends and no family. Our separate freelance careers keep us apart for 4-5 hours a day and that's plenty!*"

In summary, we do find that the attachment theory lends an important concept to our understanding of why we fall in love because it explains why those with a stronger loving relationship are more likely to not want to spend much time apart from their partner. The added use of pet names indicates that the attachment theory does add a helpful piece to the puzzle as to the cause of love.

EVOLUTIONARY THEORY

Evolutionists view almost every aspect of human behavior in terms of reproductive success.   Love is no exception.   These theorists believe that to ensure parents raise healthy children, they must first carefully select their mates favoring the following characteristics: physical attractiveness, a need for sexual exclusivity, and a desire to cohabitate.

Evolutionists postulate that men choose women on the basis of physical looks because a woman's looks are the best indicator of her reproductive success.   Women, on the other hand, they conclude, choose men by their stature or power in the community because the more powerful the men are, the more they are able to secure the best reproductively valuable resources (the best land and the healthiest food to raise a child).   A point to remember in this

Which is more appealing?

regard is that the evolutionary theorists state that our "drives" influence our behavior unconsciously.   So the conscious desires may or may not take preference over evolutionary patterns.

Love and Sex

The sex drive plays a central role in the evolutionist's view of love.   Although sex is clearly a significant way to express and share love, are these theorists correct in making sex essential to being in love?   Can people who cannot have sex still be considered in love?

The answer: love and sex are two different entities.   Love gives comfort while sex gives satisfaction.   Love is an emotion while sex is an act.   If we break down love into its basic components, we find that sex is not an essential condition for mature love to exist, although sex does play a major role in the expression of loving emotions.

Since love can exist without sex, placing sex as the basis for love puts the evolutionists on unstable ground.   Sexual impulses may be important for the development of a relationship but they do not easily explain the lasting quality of a relationship.

In terms of desiring cohabitation, 93% of the research subjects in this study live together which does support that aspect of the evolutionary theory.   Another significant part

95

of the evolutionary theory states that couples need sexual exclusivity to ensure their offspring are their own.   This implies that the choice to have a sexually exclusive relationship would be desired above others when examining the most important aspects of a relationship.   In fact, even though this choice did not score as least important, it still fell significantly below both having the relationship be an active process, and agreeing to communicate honestly.   Therefore, sexual exclusivity did show some importance in the explanation of a loving relationship, but it was not the most important factor.

When subjects were asked how they realized that they had found the right person, the results showed that Physical Attraction on the average, rated significantly lower than three other choices: Inner feeling, Similar interests, and Communication.   (This discovery does not lend support to the evolutionary theory.)

In conclusion, although trying to match

evolutionary theory to love as a bonding human experience can be a complicated and sometimes confusing undertaking; this theory does give another useful perspective in explaining certain behaviors surrounding love.

THE THEORY OF NEED COMPLEMENTARITY

The theory of need complementarity states that we fall in love because we are meeting each other's needs.   Contained within this theory are two conflicting viewpoints.   The first is the idea that love results from two partners having similar needs and therefore both are very adept at knowing what the other partner desires and is feeling.   The second view is that two partners fall in love because they each have strong points that fit in with their partner's weak points - "opposites attract."

When each of the subjects was asked "How did you realize you had found the right person?"   The surprise response: *We complement each other well* was ranked close to the very last of the choices presented (see Chapter 8).   This clearly goes against the widely accepted idea that couples in love are examples of "opposites attract."   Cherise, a housewife married for 40 years, reflected the sentiments of many of the subjects when she said: "*We grow more similar the longer we are together.   Although there are areas where one of us is strong and the other weak, there are also areas where both of us are strong or both weak and our closeness is not based on complementing each other.*"

Louis, an architect married for 25 years, put it in a similar way when he said: "*Although my partner does have strengths and qualities that I lack, I feel the key to our love is our compatibility of spirit.   By this I mean the essential way in which we approach life, including our moral and philosophical selves.   If these line up, it doesn't matter if you have many or few interests in common, but the more you have the stronger the relationship."*

Similar needs being met by both individuals is an important factor in loving relationships. But what needs are these couples talking about? I asked the subjects to clarify this point by inquiring further about what specific needs they felt were being met by their relationship.

The most frequently chosen answer was that emotional needs were being met in a loving relationship. This was followed by sexual, security, spiritual, and finally monetary needs.

RESULTS: Needs being met-- listed in order of importance by loving couples:

1) Emotional
2) Sexual
3) Security
4) Spiritual
5) Monetary

The subjects were also asked: Which of your partner's needs do you meet?   The overall pattern was similar, which lends credence to the reliability of the results.

The fact that security needs were being met was the most surprising fact because this was an isolated case where I added a category that was not mentioned in the research on love. All of the other responses were a compilation of what researchers had stated were important needs in a loving relationship.   "Security" was something that I added because it intuitively sounded right.   As it turned out it was very right because it surpassed both spiritual and monetary needs.

One subject, Jane, an artist married for 33 years, wrote: "*Security, to me, means that I am at peace and am calm when my spouse is there for me.   I'm upset or anxious if there is a disagreement or if he is gone for a long time. I wouldn't be comfortable in life without him. He is my best friend.*"

Louis, the architect and Jane's spouse, spoke about security in the following way: "*As a former rough New York City street kid, I knew that I could survive in any environment. However, through Jane's love for me, she has taught me how to flourish and that is the key to a full, joyful life.*"

Another subject, Roger, a baker married for 6 years, said: "*Security comes from knowing your partner will carry out her part of the bargain.   I know she will support me and be there when I need her, as well as when I have no special needs.*"

In sum, the research showed that emotional, sexual and security needs are about equal in terms of importance and that spiritual and monetary needs are statistically behind. Therefore, a continuing, loving relationship is essentially an emotional, sexual connection that serves to provide a secure environment for both partners.

UNIVERSAL LOVE THEORY

One way to understand the cause of love is to portray it as universal. The universal love theorists view love as an orientation of character which, when experienced, is not focused upon one individual, but, instead, emanates out from one's personality toward all people. Some of the universal love theorists qualify this

definition by saying that this does not mean that
an individual loves all people with equal
intensity, but that the experience is the same
with all people.

My research subjects were asked to
evaluate this concept.   Each subject was asked

to rate a statement by Erich Fromm, a noted theorist who represents the view of universal love, with a true or false answer to this question:

IF I TRULY LOVE ONE PERSON, THEN I LOVE ALL PERSONS, I LOVE THE WORLD, I LOVE LIFE.

A secret part of me had hoped to find that the subjects who were more in love, more balanced, and together longer would rate this statement as true more so than the opposite group.   But this did not turn out to be the case. Actually, more people rated this question as false (though by a close margin - 51% to 49%). None of the other factors (balance, love, or time spent together) influenced the answers.

This question evoked a lot of unsolicited responses from the subjects, ranging from people remarking that this was a beautiful statement, to people asking me if I was making a joke.   However, there was not a clear statement from the subjects on the topic of universal love.   This was easily the most disappointing finding of my research.   I wanted to find in this group of people - who had evolved their thinking to this spiritual plane - that there was a clear message of enlightened understanding that we all could strive for.   But I found out, once again, that life is never as simple as you want it to be.

Viewing Fromm's statement in a very rational way, Cherise, the housewife mentioned previously, was one of the subjects who disagreed with his sentiment.   She said: "*I love my husband because of who he is and because of the position he has in my life.   Just any other person, like a next door neighbor, cannot replace him or stir the same feeling of love I feel for my husband.   How can someone love a stranger, a murderer, or an enemy?*"

Viewing this statement in a positive way,

Jack, a psychologist married for 22 years, said: "*If I truly love myself, then my experience is that my cup is so overflowing that I have plenty of love for all others. If I don't love myself, then I can't love anyone else either.*" Torrie, an aerobics instructor married for 10 years, answered: "*I believe we are all pieces of a whole. Therefore, everyone, having chosen a different path or direction to take in life, is just an extension of ourselves. Since we are all extensions of ourselves and I love myself, then I love everyone - all of life. It is one and the same.*"

Although it is a positive sign that many people look at love in a spiritual way, some take it to an extreme. Their relationship can evolve into a personal religion, a means of salvation, and a purpose for living. It is easy to see how this could create an enormous demand upon a partner. The universal love theorists, although they do have a spiritual tone to their theory, are not advocating transforming one's partner into a higher power.   They simply point out that one should strive to have a loving relationship with your **self** and then this acceptance will naturally become a part of the accepting and loving way of responding to others.

The important point in looking at all of these theories is to search your inner self for the reason as to why you are in love, or want to be in love.   Your response will help you to more clearly have the loving experience that you want.

♥ ♥

CHAPTER SEVEN: LOVE: ITS PROBLEMS AND SOLUTIONS

An important factor in any relationship is the level of self-esteem of the people involved. Low self-esteem can cause problems because if you do not love yourself then the experience of someone else loving your "self" will not seem real.   Some theorists have proposed that people with lower self-esteem need more love and thus experience love as more intense. Research has shown that the opposite is true, those with higher self-esteem report experiencing mature love more frequently. Findings such as this have lead researchers to hypothesize that a high level of self-esteem is a basic requirement for love.   To test this idea, subjects were asked this question:

TO WHAT DEGREE DO YOU BELIEVE THAT YOU

ARE LOVABLE?

(A) Less than 20%

(B) 50%

(C) 75%

(D) 100%

The current research, along with the conventional wisdom, suggested that those "more in love" would choose the 100% lovable option more frequently.   However, an astonishing two-thirds of subjects chose (C), the 75 percent lovable option while only one-fourth said that they were (D) 100% lovable.   One seventh of the subjects said they were (B) 50% lovable and only one person said that they were (A) less than 20% lovable.

These percentages are much lower than the experts would lead us to expect.   Therefore, the subjects' responses show that more than half of the couples in love do not find themselves to be 100% lovable.

To further examine this issue, the subjects were asked:

HOW WOULD YOU RATE YOUR SELF-ESTEEM IN RELATION TO THE OTHER PEOPLE THAT YOU KNOW?

(A) My self esteem is higher than most of the people that I know.
(B) My self-esteem is about the same as most of the people that I know.
(C) My self-esteem is lower than most people that I know.

Less than half of those in a loving relationship said that their self-esteem was (A) Higher than the people that they knew (45%). An equal amount said that their self-esteem was (B) The same as the people that they knew

(46%), which is much lower than expected among those in a lasting, loving relationship. The lowest percentage was in the (C) Lower than category as expected (9%).

Interestingly, the subjects were also asked to rate their partner's self-esteem.   They responded with almost the same responses for each question which lends consistency to the results.

Joe, a mathematician married for 42 years, said: "*My deep inner pervading conviction is that I am lovable.   It is something I regard as basic and I nurture my self-love. I can also be hard on myself and I am learning to be more gentle.*"

From these results we find that people in love generally feel that they are only 75% lovable, and for many lovers, their self-esteem is no higher the average person.   Problems only arise when a person's self-esteem is significantly lower than average.   This often leads to insecurities and jealousy because a person with low self-esteem cannot adequately accept love from another person.   If you do not love yourself then it is difficult to believe that someone else loves you.   Fortunately, your self-esteem does not need to be exceptionally high and you do not need to love yourself 100% to function well in a mature, loving relationship.

Some theorists speculate that if a person was raised by parents who have a loving relationship, then that person is more likely to have mature, loving relationships later in life. This has been assumed for several reasons which include the fact that this person will have had positive role models, and will have been raised in a more loving environment.

To test this idea, the subjects were asked:

HOW WOULD YOU DESCRIBE YOUR PARENTS

RELATIONSHIP?

(A) They did not have a close relationship.

(B) They were together but not emotionally
close.

(C) They had a close relationship.

Even though counselors would classify
most families as dysfunctional, a surprisingly
high percentage (47%) of couples studied said (C)
Their parents had a close relationship.   Also,
when those "in love" were compared with those
"not in love," a much higher percentage of those
in love selected (C) Their Parents had a close
relationship.

The research also showed that a
combination of 53% of the parent's relationships
were either (A) Not close or (B) Not emotionally
close.   However, according to our research,
those parents that were close had a significantly

higher chance of having an offspring in a loving relationship.

Karen, a housewife married for 52 years, had a typical response similar to many of the subject's responses: "*I think my parents' relationship was very loving, with a lot of consideration and also some humor from my dad. They were both very connected to each other and to their family. They didn't seem to talk about philosophical things like love very often (at least not in my presence) but they seemed to live it.*"

It is important to note that there is research demonstrating that adults who endured disturbed parenting were able to later function in a mature relationship...they just have to work harder at recognizing and accepting their past negative experiences.

Mike, a retired maintenance employee married for 45 years, stated: "*My parents did not have a loving relationship - they divorced when I was 9.   If I have a good marriage, it's*

because we have worked at it.   No one taught

either of us about commitment, communication,

or tolerance."

My professional training instructed that

sexual issues and money were the two areas

that caused the most difficulty in relationships.

I wondered whether or not this was true for

couples in love.

The subjects were asked:

WHICH OF THE FOLLOWING HAVE CAUSED THE
MOST DISSENTION IN YOUR RELATIONSHIP?

(A) Sexual issues.

(B) Children/ Child rearing issues.

(C) Money.

(D) In-laws.

(E) Religious Values.

(F) Housework/ Chores.

(G) Partner's behaviors and habits.

Surprisingly, the results showed that (G)
Partner's behaviors and habits scored the
highest in terms of causing the most problems.
Money (C) came in second. Housework (F),
Children (B), Sexual issues (A), and In-laws (D)
were all grouped in the middle. Significantly
lower than all of the other choices was Religious
values (E).

The most surprising finding was how high
(G) Partner's Behaviors scored, and how little
difficulty (A) Sexual issues caused.

Sheryl, a teacher married for 5 years,
said: "*My husband tends to spend too much time
in the garage, and he doesn't pick up around the
house unless I leave explicit instructions.   It
drives me crazy!   Thank goodness we both have
a sense of humor or goodness knows what would
happen.*"

Karen, the housewife married for 52
years, stated that she deals with partnership

117

difficulties by communicating a lot. She further added: *"Sometimes, we'll let one another know about an appreciation and also a bug. If we do this with the small stuff, the bigger things don't seem to occur as often."*

Marriage as a Destination or a Journey

Many individuals see marriage as a final destination. They consider it a release from the pressures of single life. They consider the long list of things they did to entice and attract their partner as no longer a necessity. To some people, being married means no longer having to do a long list of "chores" to attract the opposite sex. No longer is going to the gym necessary, or doing *that* sexual act, or being romantic, or attentive...lounging around the house in dirty shirts and sweat pants is now the preferred attire. This attitude can cause the relationship to wither. Then, the need for what feels like love, attention, and sexual gratification outweighs the fear of destroying the relationship. Part of the conflict lies in the fact that both members of the couple are, after marriage, still sexual beings looking for validation, touching, excitement and fulfillment. When you combine these continued physical and emotional needs with a neglected and withered relationship, ultimately relationships become strained and often broken. These individuals often forget that the relationship is something to be nurtured and cultivated.

People are then "surprised" when their partner cheats even though all that is holding the pair together are vows spoken on their wedding day. Therefore, it is vital to find a partner who is as committed to working on the relationship as you are.

Problems within a relationship are always a matter for both partners. When individuals start saying "It's not my problem, I don't have a

Who receives more affection, your pet or your spouse?

problem, it's my partner" then the relationship loses the partnership benefit that it was designed to create.

I wanted to know -- when problems and difficulties arise, do couples in love search out assistance or do they work it out themselves?

I asked the subjects this question:

HAVE YOU BEEN IN ANY TYPE OF ORGANIZED LEARNING, SUCH AS THE FOLLOWING, THAT HAS HELPED YOU TO ENHANCE YOUR RELATIONSHIP?

(A) Individual Therapy.

(B) Marital Therapy.

(C) Seminars and Workshops.

(D) Books on Relationships or Communication.

The largest group, 44%, said that their relationship was helped by (D) Books on relationships, 26% said they had been to (C) Seminars, 24% said they had been in (A) Individual therapy and 15% said that they had been in (B) Marital therapy.

About two-thirds of the respondents indicated that they had some help in creating their successful relationship.

Maxine, married for 20 years, was asked what she does to keep her relationship strong? "*We have plenty of sex!*"

Pete, a retired military officer married for 39 years, claimed: "*About two years after we were married, we went to a weekend seminar on communication for couples. While there, we learned self-disclosure skills and listening skills. This was marvelous for our relationship to share at both positive times as well as when we have an issue to work through.*"

In regard to relationship problems, a very wise woman, my grandmother, once said, "It's not whether you have problems that's important, it's how quickly you work them out and get back to being in love." The couples in lasting, loving relationships did not say that they did not have problems, they just said they made it a priority to work them out.

♥ ♥

CHAPTER EIGHT: FINDING LOVE IN A CULTURE FILLED WITH INFIDELITY AND DIVORCE

From politicians, to music and sports icons, to movie stars, to religious leaders--infidelity is spreading unchecked through our "role models" and our current culture.   It is becoming harder to fool ourselves into believing that this lapse in judgment and confusion about loving relationships is only happening to our heroes.   One of the most important lessons from this *Report* will be for all of us to understand and learn how to rise above this cultural wave of relationship misunderstanding.

Infidelity causes severe damage to a relationship and is often one of the hardest problems for a couple to move past.   Over a long-term relationship, the temptation to cheat is likely to attack a weakened relationship at some point.   So I wanted to know how couples in love dealt with this potential problem. Would the partners have such a close, secure relationship that they could discuss the problematic temptation with each other, or would this be pushing the limits of intimate communication?

The couples were asked the following question:

WOULD YOU TELL YOUR PARTNER IF YOU FELT LIKE HAVING AN AFFAIR AND THAT THIS THOUGHT WAS CAUSING YOU DISTRESS?

(A) Never.

(B) Most likely not.

(C) If it was a problem for me, then I would discuss it with my partner.

Surprisingly, more than half of the couples, 56%, felt comfortable enough to (C) Discuss this extremely difficult problem with their partner. Only 26% said (B) Most likely not and 18% said (A) Never.

All of this potentially destructive behavior leads to one conclusion - that everyone who wants a lasting connection needs to learn how to nurture a loving relationship by communicating even their deepest concerns to make the relationship last.

Someone Old or Someone New?

Today, anybody—married or not-- can open a website, quickly find a personal section, and with hardly any effort -- get a date.   But let's say you go out to a fancy restaurant and have "the perfect time" with "the perfect extremely attractive person."   Does that mean you should start applying the principles found in this *Report*?   Should you **instantly** decide that you have found your mate, or should you keep

dating others to make sure?   (If you are

cheating, should you drop your current

relationship and move to the new "exciting"

one?)   To discover when individuals in lasting,

loving relationships felt they had found the right

person—someone they could truly trust,

subjects were asked:

DID YOU FALL IN LOVE...

(A) At first sight?

(B) On the first day or night?

(C) After a few times together?

(D) After months of knowing each other?

The results showed that love at first sight

did not turn into a mature, loving relationship.

Ninety percent of the subjects in this research

said that they did not fall in love at first sight.

And more than a third of the subjects said that it took **months** before they knew they were in love.

This is something to remember.

Although the experience of the initial attraction may be very intense, and in fact may continue for quite some time, this is not the same experience as mature love. It is a strong admiration for an unknown person which is frequently proportional to the amount of loneliness experienced before the "love at first sight" occurred. This is infatuation. (A thorough discussion of infatuation is in Chapter 9.)

This research concludes that love develops over time. For instance, Randy, a construction worker, stated: "*I didn't experience love at first sight with Jo. It was after knowing one another for about 8 months that I had grown to love her, and that love has continued to grow ever since.*"

"I just met the perfect man and the crazy guy already wants to marry me!"

A *Love Report* subject, who did not want her name mentioned, said: "*I did not experience love at first sight, but rather a strong interest. I probably felt in love after a few months, but I also had an intuition that he was the one*."

Mack, a mechanic married for 49 years, stated: "*We have known each other since we were very young (7 or 8 years old). I always*

liked Rosy.   In my later years (15 to 19), I knew I
was in love.   As we spent more and more time
together, we shared our thoughts, our faith, our
plans and our dreams. I'm sure I was infatuated,
but only as a part of the process of our growing
love."

Have You Found Your Soul Mate?

What are you to do if you don't feel
completely satisfied with your chosen partner?
How can you tell for sure that you have found
the right person?   Maybe your partner is not
your real "soul mate?"   Are you denying
yourself a union with your true partner by
remaining in your current relationship?   If you
are not completely satisfied, should you try for
something better?   Or should you stay with
what you have?

Subjects were asked to discuss how they decided that they had found the right person with the following question:

HOW DID YOU REALIZE THAT YOU HAD FOUND THE RIGHT PERSON?

(A) We have similar values, interests and goals.

(B) We have never been with anyone better.

(C) We just had an inner feeling that we were the right person for each other.

(D) We are able to communicate and understand each other at deep levels.

(E) We had a physical attraction for each other.

(F) We complement each other well.

I thought that (C) An inner feeling would steal the show; this was only partly accurate. Three responses tied for first place: (A) We have similar values, interests, and goals, (C) Had an inner feeling and (D) We are able to communicate and understand each other at deep levels.

Again, communication turned out to be paramount in the loving couples' relationship. (E) Physical attraction was found to be less important; followed by (F) We complement each other well; and finally (B) Never been with anyone better, in that order.

If you are saying to yourself that the reason you are in love is because you are extremely sexually attracted to this person, and you have not found anyone better, then you are using the wrong reasons as the basis for your lasting, loving relationship.

QUESTION FOR YOU, THE READER:

HOW CAN YOU TELL IF YOU FOUND THE RIGHT PERSON FOR A LASTING, LOVING RELATIONSHIP?

"He's everything I could possibly hope for, but I don't think I'm in love."

1) Do you have an inner feeling that this is the right person?

2) Are you able to communicate and understand each other at deep levels?

3) Do you have similar interests, values and goals?

4) Is your partner willing to discuss and agree to a commitment?

If you can answer "Yes!" to those basic questions then congratulations, you are on the right track toward finding the right person for a lasting, loving relationship.

One of the subjects, Roger, a commercial pilot married for 34 years, talked about his inner feeling when he believed he had found the right person: *"I knew I found the right person when I realized I wanted to be with her all the time... I wanted to come home to her and have her share my successes and failures..."*

This research has shown that you can tell if you have found the right person...if you have an inner feeling that this person is the right one...if you both have similar values, interests and goals...you both communicate well...**and** if you are both willing to make a commitment to the relationship.   This information is crucial and needs to be employed for couples to find, create, and sustain love.

Accordingly, you can be prepared for love by understanding the meaning of love, by knowing when you have found love, and by valuing the importance of maintaining a communicative and loving relationship.

CHAPTER NINE:
THE NEW DEFINITION
OF LOVE

One way to begin a definition is to point out what it is not.   If I can clarify the definitions that are masquerading as love, then the real definition of mature love will be easier to see. Some love theorists have defined love as the painful/joyful experience associated with falling in love or more correctly infatuation.   This involves the experience of not knowing a person fully.

The word love should not be used to describe a relationship until both partners can say that they know each other well enough to know the good and bad side of their partner. Before that, the experience is simply an unrealistic, passionate, idealization.

By discarding the negative connotation associated with infatuation, we can experience it in a more realistic way, as a wonderful,

exciting, and often frequently painful experience.

People need to be comfortable saying: "I am

infatuated with the amazing, terrific, sexy

person I met last week" instead of "I just fell

madly in love!" The second statement is false.

When these two different experiences are

corrected in our language, then they will

become clearer in our thinking and also in the

way we approach our relationships.

With so many people asking "Why

doesn't love last?" they could instead be asking,

"Why doesn't infatuation last?" The answer

would then be simple. Infatuation does not

last because infatuation involves not knowing a

person fully. As the infatuation progresses, the

infatuated person inevitably learns more about

the idealized person. This person will

eventually be found to have human failings and

to that extent the infatuation dies.

The word love can also be misused in more harmful ways than just confusing it with infatuation. Some people have confused love so completely that a destructive relationship can result even when a person believes that he or she is "in love." For example, when the need to dominate, manipulate, or control another person is the paramount reason for maintaining a relationship, then it not loving, it is exploitive. This type of relationship needs to be recognized for what it is...not a mature loving relationship. A person who says, "I am staying with my partner who abuses me because I am in love," has terribly confused the meaning of the word love.

If a relationship is based entirely upon satisfying one's own needs to the extent that the partner's needs are neglected, then that is not an experience of loving the other person. Rather, it is an attempt at self-love thinly disguised as real love. By the same token, if giving to one's partner is based on the expectation of receiving something back in the future, then it is not a real giving of one's self. Again, it is an attempt at self-love that is doomed to fail.

Love is sometimes also used as an excuse for not dealing with the larger questions of life. Energy that may have naturally fostered spiritual pursuits is transferred to the relationship. The relationship is then expected to provide a spiritually awakening experience. Love can then become over-burdened with unrealistic expectations, and if it comes up short, people begin asking: "Will I ever find true love?"

We all need to help promote an informed use of the word love so people do not confuse other actions and emotions for mature love. A statement such as "I love my wife *and* I love my girlfriend" can no longer be tolerated. If anything, it must be changed to "I lust after my girlfriend and I feel safe with my wife."

In this day and age when love is forming the sole basis of our relationships and thus the essential building blocks for our society; we must declare love as a bond.   The time has come for our culture to evolve past the conception of love as an exciting sensation that overwhelms us with desire.   We do not need to deny the passion of infatuation, but rather delegate it to its proper place.

Love as a Human Experience

The question that is significant to ask is: "What is love?"   As a human experience, love is not something that can easily be put into words - just as the experience of being "happy" is difficult to explain.   Therefore, the following is an attempt to define the components of a couples' loving experience (based on couples in love) so that all of us who are trying to attain this experience for ourselves can have a better conceptual understanding of what it is that we are seeking.

DEFINITION OF LOVE:

Love is an emotional, sexual and security-creating experience between two people that grows over time and results from making a commitment to the process of sharing yourself, understanding your partner, and actively participating in making the relationship better.

Once this definition is understood and followed, the benefits of a long-term relationship will blossom naturally.   The warm experience of caring and being cared for, learning about your "self," having a close intimate connection - all the benefits of a mature loving relationship - grow when this is

140

the foundation of your relationship.

In conclusion, there are two main findings that have grown out of *The Love Report* research.   The first is that love and infatuation need to be separated in all aspects

of our culture.   They must be separated in our minds, our language, and in the way that we view our relationships.   The second significant finding is that love is based upon commitment -

a commitment to our partners and a
commitment to the process of our relationships.
The fabric of our society is based upon these
fragile commitments and it is essential that our
perspective and understanding come into
alignment with the enormous importance we
have placed upon love.

♥ ♥

CHAPTER TEN: THE ROME SCALE

Relationship

Openness

Maturity

Evaluation

This test will help you evaluate your knowledge and readiness to enjoy a lasting, loving relationship.   It emphasizes the key messages that couples in love say are important to understand to achieve the benefits of true love.

True / False questions:

1._____ You know immediately when you meet your true soul mate.

2._____ You cannot be in love unless you are having sex.

3._____ The experience of love hasn't changed in thousands of years.

4._____ You must come from a healthy childhood to have a normal love life.

5._____ When you are really in love, you tell your partner everything.

6._____ Couples in love reach a stage where they communicate unconsciously.

7._____ Couples in love need to take vacations away from each other to keep things fresh.

8._____ Commitment means you will stay together no matter what.

9._____ Being in love means that you and your partner don't have secrets.

10._____ "Opposites Attract" describes the relationships that last.

11._____ Loving couples treat each other childishly at times.

12._____ You have to love yourself completely before you can love someone else.

13._____ Romance and sex are the primary components of love.

14._____If you meet the right person, you can fall in love right away.

15._____ Sexual issues are the primary problems for relationships.

16._____ Infatuation is immature.

17._____ Love fades with time.

18._____ If you have doubts about your new partner, then you probably have not found your soul mate.

19._____ The more educated you are, the more likely it is that you are in love.

20._____ If you can look at your partner and say that you have never been with anyone better then that means you are in love.

21._____ Finding a person to love today is much easier than it was in the past.

22._____ True love involves an active participation in making the relationship better.

STOP and write down your answers before continuing.

ANSWERS

All answers are based upon couples who were participants in *The Love Report* research: (Note: Questions 11 and 22 are true; the rest are false.)

1. If you meet your true soul mate, then you can tell right away.   False.

Most of the couples in love said that they did not experience "love at first sight." They had an initial attraction that built into an experience of love over time. Once they got to know each other in a deep sense and they still were attracted to each other, then they came to have a strong inner feeling that their partner was "the right one."

2. You cannot be in love unless you are having sex.   False.

People who abstain from sex can still be

in love.   Although the sexual expression

of love is very important for many people,

the act of sex and the emotion of love

are separate.

3. The experience of love hasn't changed

in thousands of years.   False.

Every generation has its own definition

of love.   Our generation's way of

looking at love needs to evolve so that

the expression "the love of my life" takes

on real importance and meaning in our

current society.

4. You must come from a healthy childhood to have a normal love life. False.

Although it is true that you are more likely to be in a loving relationship if you were raised in a loving family, the research on love shows that with extra effort, people who come from highly dysfunctional families can have a healthy, loving relationship.

5. When you are really in love, you tell your partner everything.   False.

This is not true because while couples in love are very self-disclosing and vulnerable with their partners, they tend to hold back saying things that would be hurtful.   They are not always 100%

open and direct; they censure themselves.

6. Couples in love reach a stage where they communicate unconsciously. False.

While couples who spend a lot of time together do have strong, almost unconscious sense of what their partner is thinking and feeling, couples in love make it a habit to talk about issues regularly, especially whenever they become distressed.

7. Couples in love need to take vacations away from each other to keep things fresh.   False.

Couples in lasting, loving relationships generally do not enjoy being apart.

They usually spend the majority of their free time together.

8. Being committed to your partner means that you will stay together no matter what.   False.

When the couples in love defined commitment, they chose "stay together no matter what" as the LAST way that they would define their commitment.   It was much more important for them to agree to work on building the relationship in an active way.   Agreeing to communicate openly and honestly was also very important.

9. Being in love means that you and your partner don't have secrets.   False.

Seventy percent of the couples in love would disagree with this statement. They believe that there are things in the past that are better left in the past.

10. "Opposites Attract" describes the relationships that last.   False.

Couples in lasting relationships emphasize their similarities much more than their differences.   They state that they have similar interests, values, and goals while putting "We complement each other well" last among the descriptions of their relationship.

11. Loving couples treat each other childishly at times.   True.

This is true. Loving couples treat each other the same as a mother would treat a young child. They copy the mannerisms and gestures with each other similar to the way that a baby is handled and cared for.

12. You have to love yourself completely before you can love someone else.
False.

This is not true. Many of the couples in this research stated that their self-esteem was not any higher than the other people that they knew and that they could be very self-critical. However, having an exceptionally low self-esteem can cause problems because if you can't have any love for yourself then it is hard to believe that someone else can.

13. Romance and sex are the primary components of love.   False.

This is absolutely not true.   Romance and sex are the primary components of infatuation, not love.   This distinction needs to be clearly made.   Real, lasting love is based upon commitment, self-disclosure, and an active participation in making the relationship work.

14. If you meet the right person, you can fall in love right away.   False.

This is absolutely not true.   Love is an emotion that develops over time after getting to know a person in a deep, close way.

15. Sexual issues are the primary problems for relationships.   False.

Surprisingly, this is not the case. Couples in love report that their partner's habits and money issues cause the most problems in the long run.

16. Infatuation is immature.   False.

It is important to avoid looking at infatuation as something negative.   It is a natural process that occurs as a result of deep needs.   If we can look at infatuation in a positive light then maybe it won't become so confused with love.

17. Love fades with time.   False.

This is not true.   True love between two committed people who are actively working on their relationship grows with time.   I have met many happy, loving, long-lasting couples who make their relationship a priority and are rewarded with untold treasures.

18. If you have doubts about your new partner, then you probably have not found your soul mate.   False.

If you have no doubts about somebody who you have just met, then you fit into the infatuation group.   The romance novels put forth the "love at first sight" idea.   Unfortunately, it leads many people to be disappointed.

19. The more educated you are, the more likely it is that you are in love. False.

Education levels do not influence the strength of love.

20. If you can look at your partner and say that you have never been with anyone better, then that means you are in love.   False.

It takes much more than that to be in love.   Unfortunately, many couples feel that since they have not been with anyone better, their experience must be love.

21. Finding a person to love today is much easier than it was in the past. False.

Finding a partner in today's society can be accomplished once you clearly understand the meaning of love. How hard it is to find love changes as the definition has changed over time.

22. True love involves an active participation in making the relationship better. True.

As with anything that grows, a loving relationship needs nurturing.

Scoring:

22-19 correct = You are open to a lasting, loving relationship.

18-15 correct = You are on the right track but there are a few issues to consider.

14-0 correct = Your ideas differ from couples in lasting, loving relationships

Take these questions and answers not as absolute, but as ideas to stimulate your thinking.

♥ ♥

CHAPTER 11: LESSONS LEARNED ABOUT LOVE

1) Understand the difference between love and lust.   Keep these two separated in your thoughts, your words, and your actions.

2) Understand clearly what you mean when you say "I am in love."   Write down exactly what that statement means to you.

3) If you define love as something that happens "at first sight," then don't be surprised when it disappears just as quickly.

4) When you are in a relationship, the deeper you share your intimate self, the deeper love you will create.

5) Discuss with your partner exactly what you both mean by a *relationship commitment.*

6) Realize that nobody is perfect and we are all on this journey together.

7) If you take the lessons in *The Love Report* to heart, you will be ready to find, create, nurture and enjoy your own loving relationship.

APPENDIX #1

SAMPLES OF SOME OF *THE LOVE REPORT* COUPLES:

Traci and Lou married for 15 years

Traci, who works as an interior designer, said that she liked her husband Lou from the first time she saw him in the gym.   "*I tried to remain 'in like' with him until he said, 'I love you' (that was 3 or 4 months).   We are like spirits and we believe in never going to sleep at night until all issues are resolved and we have made up and kissed.*"

"*I did not experience love at first sight or infatuation,*" said Lou.   "*It took nearly 2 years before I felt 'in love' with her.   Most of the people that I know say their relationship is more important than their career and then they turn around and only spend 20 minutes a day (maybe) with their partner. My relationship with Traci has become the center of my universe.   Since I consider my relationship to be part of my essence, I make my life choices spring from that essence.*"

Joel and Sheri married for 28 years

Sheri, a housewife, said: "*I knew he was right because he became my best friend.   I think we are similar in our basic values but our interests are different enough.   He is a furniture refinisher and I am working on becoming an optometrist.   Our differences mean we have things to talk about.   When I feel down, I don't feel loveable.   But when I am up (most of the time) my self-esteem is better than most. I find it difficult to overcome my early childhood experiences where I didn't feel lovable.   We don't take each other or the relationship for granted.   Complacency equals certain death.*"

Joel, a retired engineer, said: "*The feeling of being in love didn't hit me until we were living together.   I enjoyed being in lust but lust doesn't keep a relationship alive.   I think being in love began after the lust began to tarnish.   I could talk about Sheri's habits but I won't.   Nobody's perfect and in close proximity anybody would be annoying sometimes. However, a willingness to discuss problems, to face my own inadequacies, and to compromise helps to keep our love*

alive."

<u>Ruth and Saul married for 36 years</u>

Ruth is a church secretary.   She was raised in the
Midwest and had never been out of the country.   Saul was
raised in Israel and works as a general contractor.   Ruth:
"We met in college at a gathering for international students.
We danced together most of the evening and he walked home
with me, and talked the entire mile and a half.   In later years
I joked that I only understood one word in ten.   I can still
almost taste the physical attraction I felt when I looked at his
shoulders in the first two years we knew each other!   And
yet I find him more attractive now than I did then, in spite of
increasing age!   One of the things that especially endeared
him to me was that he communicated feelings and thoughts
he had never expressed before.   He once cried while we were
talking on the phone, and I felt that was a breakthrough in
our relationship, and that I could trust myself in a relationship

with a man who was willing to risk that degree of self-disclosure."

Saul, a retired doctor, said: "*Basically we have just muddled through.   If there are any rules, they were that we stuck together through everything, the downs as well as the ups, doing the best we could.   This has included having very little money to start; raising four children, planned and unplanned as to timing, designing and building the house we live in - still unfinished after 16 years; surviving unemployment, cancer surgery, and taking care of our incapacitated parents.   Through it all, and it wasn't as bad as it sounds, we have had a wonderful life of love, work and travel.   In spite of all the time and effort that we put into our marriage, I often feel it is like raising children: you do the best you can, but it is the grace of God and a lot of good fortune if it all turns out all right.   We have been truly blessed.*"

♥ ♥

APPENDIX #2

THE HISTORY OF MARRIAGE VOWS

In *The Love Report*, commitment was found to be extremely important to the couples in love. Since the marital vows are the written form of that commitment, this topic will be examined in detail.

The marriage vows may be the single most important collection of statements that a person makes in his or her lifetime. Even so, most people do not have a clear understanding about how or why the vows were developed, what they symbolize, or what they actually mean.

It is a common belief that the momentous commitment "*to love and to honor, till death do us part*" is taken directly from the Bible. In fact, both the Christian Bible and the Jewish Talmud do not contain marriage vows. Instead, they developed from a complicated history of influences derived from many sources, all of which have reflected the prevalent society's beliefs about relationships and marriage.

The earliest marriages were "marriage by capture." These marriages consisted of a man sneaking into a neighboring tribe and absconding with a young woman. The man would then proceed to hide out during their "honeymoon" until the bride's family search was discontinued.   During these early days, living together for a short period of time was all that was needed for a marriage to be considered valid.   These "capture marriages" led to many wars and violent disagreements between tribes.   The dowry was therefore invented to quell the anger of the tribe that had lost their young female.   The consent of the woman's parents soon became a requirement for marriage because the parents were the ones to provide the dowry.

As towns became established, people looked to religious manuals for guidance.   The earliest manuals (or "Rites" as they were called) were designed to move the society toward a more civilized way of life.   These manuals attempted to shift away from the practice of marriage by capture by proclaiming that a woman's consent was needed for a marriage to take place.   For instance, in the Latin Rite both spouses were declared to be the ministers of the

168

ceremony and their consent alone was necessary for the marriage to be valid.   In 1125, Bury St. Edmunds, in his English Rite, declared that the bride and groom's consent had to be declared publicly.   No longer was consent assumed just from the fact that the marriage was taking place.

The early Christian Church Fathers frowned upon marriage.   They considered virginity as the perfect way to serve God.   In fact, the early ceremonies that did take place contained readings from the Bible extolling celibacy and warning against fornication.   But since so many marriages continued to occur, and since so many Christians were not following the ideal of virginity, the Church eventually shifted toward a more accepting view of marriage.   Marriage was chosen as the place to reflect God's love and the mechanism by which Christians were commanded to "go forth and multiply" - though sex was only intended for procreation.

The early Church ceremonies emphasized the creation of offspring.   In the ninth century, the Bobbio Missal, a mass-book of Irish-Spanish origins, contained the first mention of the "Blessing of the bedchamber over those being married."   This blessing gained central importance in most early ceremonies for the purpose of helping young couples to produce many healthy children.

Problems arose when men began to secretly marry many women simultaneously to enrich themselves with the many dowries.   Thus the earliest religious vows incorporated the requirement that "banns" (or notices) be placed in the churches of both the bride and the groom for eight days.   During the ensuing ceremony, the parish members were required to "*speak now or forever hold your peace,*" which included speaking up if they knew that either the bride or groom was already married, or if a member of the parish had knowledge that the bride was being married against her will, or if one of the bridal couple was below the required age (14 for boys and 12 for girls).

During the twelfth century, in a rite written by Bury St. Edmunds, the vows were joined with the symbolic giving of rings.   The ring was placed on the thumb with the words "*in the Name of the Father*" then transferred to the index finger saying "*the Son*" and then left on the middle finger saying "*the Holy Spirit.*"   The groom then said "*with this ring I thee wed, this gold and silver I give thee, with my body I thee* honor, with this dowry I thee endow," and then the bride fell to her knees as a sign of obedience.   When there were less women available, the requirement to provide the dowry shifted from the woman's family, to the man's.   A similar set of early vows appeared in the twelfth century from the Magdalen Pontifical that stated to the groom: "*Do you wish to serve her in the faith of God as your own, in health and infirmity, as a Christian man should serve his wife?*"

In the thirteenth century, the Roman rite combined these early statements into the first true vows of consent: "*Do you really want this woman as your wife, to guard her in health and sickness, as long as she lives, as a good man should keep his wife, and to join her faithfully with your body, and all your possessions?*"   These early Roman and Latin manuals (or missals as they were called) were translated into Old English and in particular, two English Missals became very important influences on the proper religious marital etiquette - The York and Sarum Missals.

The York Missal's vows sounded like this: "*Here I take thee, N. (the names were inserted in place of the capital N.) to my wedded wife, to have and to hold at bed and at board, for fairer and for fouler, for better for worse, in sickness and in health, till death us do part and thereto I plight thee my troth"* (troth means faithfulness).   The groom continued: "*With this ring I wed thee, and with this gold and silver I honour thee, with this gift I dowe thee, and with my body I thee worship.*"

Although the vows spoken today sound similar to the ones found in these early Missals - there is some potential for confusion in the translation.   For instance, one of the vows required at the marriage ceremony in the Sarum Missal was: "*to be bonere and buxom in bedde.*"   Although this sounds sexual to our modern ear, when the Old English is properly translated, it sounds quite different.   Bonere meant to be good-natured and obedient, buxom meant to be humble, gentle and submissive, and finally bedde referred to the marital relationship (the marital bed became a synonym for the marital relationship).

In 1549, many sources including these early Missals, were joined together into the *Book of Common Prayer*.   This manual excluded many of the earlier statements, such as the Sarum requirement "*to be bonere and buxom in bedde.*"
The bride's vows now sounded like this: "*I, N. take thee N. to my wedded husband, to have and to hold from this day forward, for better, for worse, for richer, for poorer, in sickness, and in health, to love, cherish (sic), and to obey* (men didn't have to say obey), *till death us depart: according to God's holy ordinance: And thereto I give thee my troth.*   The bride continued, "*With this ring I thee wed: This gold and silver I thee give: with my body I thee worship: and with all my worldly goods I thee endow.*"   These vows were repeated by the groom and then the priest would add, "*and forsaking all others, keep thee only unto him, so long as you both shall live?*"   The proper response was, "*I will.*"

The vows changed very little throughout the many revisions of the *Book of Common Prayer*.   Even so, the modern 1977 version of the *Book* has a few notable changes.

For instance, the modern vows left out the requirements that

the bride says she will obey her husband and pass all of her

worldly goods to him.   Other notable changes include the

insertion of the name of Jesus Christ in the vows.   The

marriage vows today are reflected in the example set by the

royal couple in 2011.

Vows of the English Royals

Kate Middleton followed the current trend and the

example of Diana, Princess of Wales, by not promising to

"obey" in her marriage vows.   The vows, which are listed

below, are taken from *The Liturgy of Solemnizing Marriage*

from *The Book of Common Prayer* (1559):

http://www.wwnorton.com/college/english/nael/17century/

topic_1/matrimon.htm.   By following this brief history of

the marriage vows, you can see how the vows have evolved

throughout history and how in our present time the royal couple has decided upon their current version.

I have presented the marriage vows as spoken in comparison to the 16th century Book of Common Prayer; what was newly added is in parentheses and what was left out is shown in the strikethrough text.   You can also watch on YouTube the unedited vows of Prince William and Catherine Middleton as they were spoken in April of 2011: http://www.youtube.com/watch?v=-RFL4iyoi4s.

Dearly beloved, we are gathered together here in the sight of God, and in the face of his congregation, to join together this man and this woman in holy matrimony, which is an honorable estate, instituted of God himself ~~of God in paradise in the time of man's innocency,~~ signifying unto us the mystical union, that is betwixt Christ and his Church: which holy estate Christ adorned and beautified with his presence and first miracle that he wrought in Cana of Galilee,

175

and is commended (in holy writ) ~~of Saint Paul~~ to be honorable among all men, and therefore is not by any to be enterprised nor taken in hand unadvisedly, lightly, or wantonly~~, to satisfy men's carnal lusts and appetites, like brute beasts that have no understanding~~, but reverently, discreetly, soberly, and in the fear of God, duly considering the causes for which matrimony was ordained.   (First, it was ordained for the increase of mankind according to the will of God and that children might be brought up in the fear and nurture of the Lord, and to the praise of his holy name.) ~~One was, the procreation of children to be brought up in the fear and nurture of the Lord, and praise of God.~~ Secondly, (it was ordained in that the order of the natural instincts and affections implanted by God should be hallowed and directed aright that those who are called of God to this holy estate should continue therein in pureness of living) ~~for a remedy against sin, and to avoid fornication, that such persons as have not the gift of continency [self-restraint] might marry,~~

~~and keep themselves undefiled members of Christ's body~~.

Thirdly, (it was ordained) for the mutual society, help, and comfort that the one ought to have of the other, both in prosperity and adversity: into which holy estate these two persons present come now to be joined.

Therefore, if any man can show any just cause why they may not lawfully be joined together, let him now speak.   Or else hereafter hold his peace.

I require and charge you both {as you will answer at the dreadful day of judgment, when the secrets of all hearts shall be disclosed} that if either of you do know any impediment why ye may not be lawfully joined together in matrimony, ye do now confess it.   For be ye well assured, that so many as be coupled together otherwise than God's word doth allow, are not joined together by God, neither is their matrimony lawful.

Archbishop of Canterbury to Prince William: William Arthur Philip Louis, wilt thou have this woman to thy wedded wife, to live together according to God's law in the holy estate of matrimony? Wilt thou love her, comfort her, honour and keep her, in sickness and in health; and, forsaking all other, keep thee only unto her, so long as ye both shall live?

He answered: I will.

Archbishop to Catherine: Catherine Elizabeth, wilt thou have this man to thy wedded husband, to live together according to God's law in the holy estate of matrimony? Wilt thou love him, comfort him, honour and keep him, in sickness and in health; and, forsaking all other, keep thee only unto him, so long as ye both shall live?

She answered: I will.

The Archbishop continued: Who giveth this woman to be married to this man?

The Archbishop receives Catherine from her father's hand.

Taking Catherine's right hand, Prince William says after the

Archbishop: I, William Arthur Philip Louis, take thee, Catherine Elizabeth to my wedded wife, to have and to hold from this day forward, for better, for worse: for richer, for poorer; in sickness and in health; to love and to cherish, till death us do part, according to God's holy law; and thereto I give thee my troth.

They loose hands. Catherine, taking Prince William by his right hand, says after the Archbishop: I, Catherine Elizabeth, take thee, William Arthur Philip Louis, to my wedded husband, to have and to hold from this day forward, for better, for worse: for richer, for poorer; in sickness and in health; to love and to cherish, till death us do part, according to God's holy law; and thereto I give thee my troth.

They loose hands. The Archbishop blessed the ring: Bless, O Lord, this ring, and grant that he who gives it and she who shall wear it may remain faithful to each other, and abide in thy peace and favour, and live together in love until their lives' end. Through Jesus Christ our Lord. Amen.

Prince William took the ring and placed it upon the fourth finger of Catherine's left hand. Prince William said after the Archbishop: With this ring I thee wed; with my body I thee honour; and all my worldly goods with thee I share: in the name of the Father, and of the Son, and of the Holy Ghost. Amen.

The congregation remained standing as the couple kneeled. The Archbishop says: Let us pray. O Eternal God, Creator and Preserver of all mankind, giver of all spiritual grace, the author of everlasting life: send thy blessing upon these thy servants, this man and this woman, whom we bless in thy name; that, living faithfully together, they may surely perform and keep the vow and covenant betwixt them made, whereof this ring given and received is a token and pledge;

and may ever remain in perfect love and peace together, and

live according to thy laws; through Jesus Christ our Lord.

Amen.

The Archbishop joined their right hands together and said:
Those whom God hath joined together let no man put

asunder.

The Archbishop addressed the congregation: Forasmuch as

William and Catherine have consented together in holy

wedlock, and have witnessed the same before God and this

company, and thereto have given and pledged their troth

either to other, and have declared the same by giving and

receiving of a ring, and by joining of hands; I pronounce that

they be man and wife together, in the name of the Father,

and of the Son, and of the Holy Ghost. Amen.

The Archbishop blessed the couple: God the Father, God

the Son, God the Holy Ghost, bless, preserve, and keep you;

the Lord mercifully with his favour look upon you; and so fill you with all spiritual benediction and grace, that ye may so live together in this life, that in the world to come ye may have life everlasting.   Amen.

*   *   *

Here is how my wife Christine and I interpreted the marriage vows for our own ceremony...

Officiant: Christine and Kevin have come here to publically declare their love for each other, ask for your support, and celebrate their good fortune with you.   Please consider how each of you are personally going to make this a special night of celebration in this beautiful setting with this amazing gathering of warm, loving and friendly people.   We ask that you take a short moment to close your eyes and consider the good times you have shared with Christine and Kevin, and also consider ways that you might be supportive to their union in the future.   If we could have a moment of silent reflection...

Officiant: The marriage vows are Christine and Kevin's way of publically declaring their love and commitment to each other.

From Christine: On this special day, I give to you in the presence of God and all those in attendance my sacred promise to stay by your side as your wife through the good times and the bad.   I promise to love you without reservation, comfort you in times of distress, honor and respect you, encourage you to achieve all of your goals, laugh with you and cry with you, grow with you in mind and spirit, always be open and honest with you, and cherish you for eternity.

Do you, Christine, take, Kevin, to be your husband, and vow

to be his constant friend, faithful partner in life, and his one true love?

(I do)

From Kevin: On this special day, I give to you in the presence of God and all those in attendance my sacred promise to stay by your side as your husband through the good times and the bad.   I promise to love you without reservation, comfort you in times of distress, honor and respect you, encourage you to achieve all of your goals, laugh with you and cry with you, grow with you in mind and spirit, always be open and honest with you, and cherish you for eternity.

Officiant: Do you, Kevin, take Christine to be your wife, and vow to be her constant friend, faithful partner in life, one true love?

(I do)

Officiant: Will you now exchange rings as reminders of your vows and symbols of your eternal love?   You may kiss the bride.   May we all send our good blessings and warm positive energy to this loving couple as I now introduce the new couple to you for the first time...

*   *   *

When you and your partner are ready, take some time to write your own marriage vows.   Don't sell yourself short and make statements that you don't deeply understand. Create vows that have real meaning for both you and your partner.

♥ ♥

SELECTED BIBLIOGRAPHY

After several years of researching love, I have come across a few excellent books on the subjects of love and lasting relationships. Below, I have listed some of the classics that may not be in the stores now, but have stood the test of time.

The Art of Loving, by Erich Fromm
This book is essential for anyone interested in the philosophical view of love.   He discusses the varying types of love and his universal conception of love.

Becoming Partners, by Carl Rogers
It is a timeless look at a brilliant man's ideas for a relationship.

*From Conflict to Caring: A Workbook for
Couples*, by Margaret and Jordan Paul
This is, as the title implies, a great workbook
for couples to work on becoming closer.

*Getting the Love You Want: A Guide for
Couples*, by Harville Hendrix
This is an excellent book for examining the
childhood influences that interfere with your
love relationship.

Living, Loving, and Learning, by Leo Buscaglia
If you haven't read anything by Leo Buscaglia
then you are in for an uplifting treat.   If you
have, then you know what I mean.

Love is Never Enough, by Aaron Beck
This is an excellent "How to" book for couples
with problems.   If you want to try being your
own couples therapist, this book is a good
place to start.

The Psychology of Love, edited by Robert Sternberg and Michael Barnes.

This book is a thorough compilation of the predominant research looking into the psychology of love.

Teach Only Love by Gerald Jampolsky

This is an uplifting book that examines love as a universal experience, which is the core of every one of us.

From the Author -- About the Book Cover:

The book cover picture seemed appropriate since a small part of my asking Christine to marry me involved my baking small cupcake-sized cheesecakes with red candy hearts on top. She said yes...so maybe they helped.

About the Author -- Dr. Kevin Grold:

Dr. Kevin Grold has created many psychological tests some of which have been recommended in two separate Dear Abby columns.   He has been the President of 1-800-THERAPIST, he has co-run with his wife, the world's largest eating disorder referral service www.edreferral.com, he also has a Ph.D. in psychology with an emphasis on love in long-term relationships.

Dr. Grold has many varied accomplishments from being a cancer advocate for his wife to producing a low-back workout system.   He has also been happily married since 1999.   His latest accomplishments can be found on his Facebook page:

facebook.com/kevin.grold

Dr. Grold has also developed **The Grold Love Test**, a Smartphone app currently available on Amazon at http://www.amazon.com/gp/product/B005UPT5DS and through other online app retailers. The Grold Love Test will help you create a graph of your relationship and will help you compare your current to your ideal love.

Made in the USA
Las Vegas, NV
29 January 2022

42561754R00111